C. S. DeCaro

DAYS OF NOAH

ISBN: 9798755156455

The TIMES IN WHICH WE ARE LIVING

Contents

Introduction

I'm not one to waist words that are meaningless to fill pages. Though this book is a short read, it's not without deep incite and a clear Biblical understanding of the times in which we are living. This book is coming from a non-traditional standpoint about the Biblical account of the days of Noah. As Bible prophecy is unfolding during our day at such a rapid pace, it's now that we can gain understanding and incite from the scriptures that until now were not able to be understood completely. God told Daniel that it would be like this during the time of the end, Daniel 12:8-10 *"...none of the wicked shall understand, but that the wise would understand."*

One very intriguing thing you will learn is that the book of Revelation reflects back to the very first book of the Bible, "Genesis," during the days of Noah in a way that is relevant to what we are going through right now; today! As we connect these dots, you will learn some information about the days of Noah that you probably haven't heard or been taught before. This will be the area of my primary focus as we walk through some of these compelling and jaw-dropping Biblically prophetic passages. We are living in the end times, and for Christians, the Bible is our navigation tool.

People recognize something isn't quite right today, the pandemic, mandates, chaos, division, and the unusual way our elected officials and governments of the world are leading right now. What's really going on? Where is all of this leading? The Days of Noah can give us some answers.

What's Really Going On?

Salvation is available to all while we live; however, the Bible says that those who take the "Mark of the Beast" are condemned even while alive. 2nd Thessalonians 2:11-12 says those will be "condemned" during the Endtime that believe in a specific "lie" that is brought about through a specific "strong delusion."

*11And for this reason God will send them **strong delusion**, that they should believe the **lie**, 12that they all may be **condemned** who did not believe the truth but had pleasure in unrighteousness.*
2nd Thessalonians 2:11-12 NKJV

The Endtime will be like the days of Noah, according to the Bible. We focus primarily on the Ark, animals, Noah's family, and God closing the Ark, all of which we can glean knowledge. However, what happened before this that caused God to bring about the flood? This will be the primary focus of our study.

*5Then the Lord saw that the **wickedness of man was great in the earth**, and that every intent of the **thoughts of his heart was only evil continually**. 6And the Lord was sorry that He had made man on the earth, and He was grieved in His heart.*
Genesis 5:6-7 NKJV

The next question would be, what caused this kind of widespread wickedness on earth that God saw as unredeemable? The answer is in the verse just prior.

*"**The Nephilim** were on the earth both in those days and afterward, when the **sons of God** came to the daughters of mankind, and they bore children to them. Those were the **mighty men of old, men of renown**." Genesis 6:4 NASB*

These children that were born were not human in the sense that God had created humankind as. They were part human and part demonic Nephilim. During the days of Noah, Satan made a direct attack on the image of God's crown jewel of creation, Man. Therefore the fingerprints of God through human genes (or DNA) were changed in a way to reflect satan's handy-work on every offspring that was born during those days from these women who had sexual relations with these fallen angels *(son's of God)*. By doing so, the earth was filled with a race of evil famous, influential, powerful beings to the point that evil prevailed among the humanity God created.

You may be asking, where does it say that fallen angels were the ones having relations with women on earth? It says "sons of God." When trying to get a complete understanding of Bible prophecy or anything in scripture for that matter, it's a good idea to see if other accounts in the Bible can help fill in some answers so that you can get a complete picture by bringing them together. To answer this question, let's look at the book of Job.

6Now there was a day when ***the sons of God*** *came to present themselves before the Lord,* ***and Satan also came among them****. 7And the Lord said to Satan, "From where do you come?" So Satan answered the Lord and said, "From going to and fro on the earth, and from walking back and forth on it." Job 1:6-7*

Here in the book of Job we find that satan has approached God in heaven along with the "sons of God." Satan was permitted to tempt Job, who was back on earth. What we know here is that satan wasn't alone. Satan himself is an angel. The "sons of God" were in heaven as well, approaching God's throne. These "sons of God" were not earthly. They were with satan as his angelic followers. This is how we know that Genesis 6:4 was referring to fallen angels who caused these women to birth children unlike any other on the planet, Nephilim, the Giants.

I believe Satan is up to his old tricks again now, just like in the days of Noah, and that's why the Bible describes the Endtime as such. He is just going about it differently. Satan wants to change and distort everything that God has created that reflects God. For example, Satan has attacked families with the legalization of gay marriage. Satan has even tried to claim the rainbow through LGBTQ. When you see a rainbow, it's like that's the first thing you think of. Transgenderism is a form of human mutilation. God says he has written his name in Jerusalem. That's precisely where the final battle will take place, the
"Battle of Armageddon." The list goes on. Satan's primary target has always been God's crown Jewel of creation that reflects the direct image of God, mankind.

The Mark of the Beast is described as a multi-facet implementation mechanism that will allow you to function in the economy. We know that it will consist of a "Mark" and pledge system that will require worship to an image of the Antichrist (Revelation 13).

15He was granted power to give breath to the image of the beast, that the image of the beast should both speak and cause as many as would not ***worship the image of the beast*** *to be killed.*
16He causes all, both small and great, rich and poor, free and slave, to receive a ***mark*** *on their* ***right hand*** *or on their* ***foreheads****, 17and that* ***no one may buy*** *or* ***sell*** *except one who has the* ***mark*** *or the name of the beast, or the number of his name. 18Here is wisdom. Let him who has understanding calculate the number of the beast, for it is the number of a man: His number is* ***666****. Revelation 13:15-18 NKJV*

However, as I eluded to in my previous book, ***"The Endtime is Now: According to the Bible, Be Ready!"***, the Mark of the Beast appears to consist of a pharmaceutical composition that could be a future vaccine of some sort. Since writing the book, I've become more convinced than ever, like in the Days of Noah, that this is satan's plan in attacking humanity once again at the genetic DNA fingerprint level of God's crown jewel of creation. It's going to be through a series of synthetic vaccines that will end with the final vaccine, the end-all of vaccines, the last one you will ever need. I'm sure this is how it will be pitched anyway. Since writing the book, I've discovered some additional scriptural information that I believe re-enforces this thought.

Following the 6th Trumpet war of Revelation 9 that kills one-third of humankind, we find the response from mankind in verses 20-21.

"The rest of the people, who were not killed by these plagues, did not repent of the works of their hands to stop worshiping demons and idols of gold, silver, bronze, stone, and wood, which are not able to see, hear, or walk. And they did not repent of their murders, their ***sorceries****, their sexual immorality, or their thefts." Revelation 9:20-21 NKJV*

First off, what I find interesting that's overlooked is that immediately following this war, the antichrist is not yet revealed publicly. We know this because mankind is rebuked for worshiping everything but the antichrist. After this war, they will be looking for human answers that will result in the ushering in and rise of the antichrist. Having said that, there will be a remnant of people that will know "that I'm the Lord their God" found in Ezekiel 38-39:6 that also describes aspects of this war. During Daniel's 70th week (the final seven-year period), there will also be a Great Revival.

The word "Sorceries" used here in verse 21 of Revelation 9, the original language of the Greek New Testament, is the Greek word "Pharmakeia." Pharmakeia means "drugs." This appears five times in the New Testament. We also get our English word pharmacy from the Greek word Pharmakeia. In Revelation 18:23, we find the same meaning for the word sorcery again.

*".....For your **merchants** were the great men of the earth, for by your **sorcery** all the nations were **deceived.** Revelation 18:23 NKJV*

The context here is about the headquarters of the False Prophet, "Mystery Babylon," being destroyed at the end of the tribulation period; however, there is a reflection moment made here. Notice that "all" nations were "deceived" by sorcery "Pharmakeia." Interestingly, according to the strong's concordance, the context in which it's used in the original Greek is *"the use or administering of drugs."* By replacing the word sorcery with its actual Greek usage in Revelation 18:23, it would read like this:

*".....For your **merchants** were the great men of the earth, for by your **administering of drugs** all the nations were **deceived.**" Revelation 18:23*

The "strong delusion" and "lie" of
2nd Thessalonians 2:11-12 would not contradict this. I believe the lie started in 2020 and will be restated and repeated constantly until the fulfillment of this grand lie from the father of lies that culminates with the "Mark of the beast." The merchants (businesses) are being used today to perpetrate this lie along with their government leaders of the world. This couldn't have been pulled off 2,000 years ago when this was written, however for the first time in history we see all nations in lockstep today with Pharmakeia (false vaccine) for the purpose of deceiving not healing.

Look at Revelation 16:1-2, the 1st Bowl of God's wrath that occurs towards the end of the great tribulation.

"1Then I heard a loud voice from the temple saying to the seven angels, "Go and pour out the ***bowls of the wrath of God*** *onto the earth." 2So the* ***first*** *went and poured out his bowl upon the earth, and a* ***foul and loathsome sore*** *came upon the* ***men who had the mark of the beast and those who worshiped his image."*** *Revelation 16:2 NKJV*

This gives us a timeline of when God's wrath will be poured out on humanity. God's wrath doesn't begin until after the administering of the Mark of the Beast. As I've mentioned in my previous book, ***"The Endtime is Now: According to the Bible, Be Ready!"*** because foul-smelling sores come upon people who take the "Mark of the Beast," it appears to be a pharmaceutical or medical reaction that causes these effects. This is why we can connect the dots between the "Mark of the Beast" and a pharmaceutical vaccine. What's interesting is that when you take this "Mark," you are forever condemned even though you still may live physically. I understand that there is a pledge to the Antichrist that's a part of this "Mark." However, lost people today worship all kinds of false gods, including satan himself but can still be converted to Christ, who is the TRUTH. It's only during the Endtime when people take the "Mark" that they become forever condemned. For example, during the tribulation period prior to the Mark of the Beast being administered, people will be worshiping in this one world religion led by the false prophet and worship the Antichrist. But God saves many out of this false religion right before the Mark of the Beast is administered (Revelation 18:4, also point #10 in my previous book).

And I heard another voice from heaven saying, ***"Come out of her my people"****, lest you share in her sins, and* ***lest you receive of her plaques.*** *Revelation 18:4 NKJV*

This may sound shocking to you, but I believe after taking the complexity of what this "Mark" intel's that just like in the Days of Noah, Satan tampers with God's fingerprints of human DNA which in turn, after the administering of this final piece of the puzzle (false vaccine) that it converts you into something other than what God had initially created humankind as on molecular DNA level. Therefore becoming forever condemned and unable to undo. You may not think a simple shot or series of shots could do something like changing your DNA; however, this first synthetic vaccine being administered today does add messenger "m" to your RNA (mRNA), which works closely with your DNA. For example, if you cut yourself, your DNA tells your RNA that there is a problem to be fixed. Furthermore, Transgender people take a series of shots that work to reconstruct their hormones and balances, etc.

A lot of Christians have been contemplating whether to take this particular vaccine or not. Some are struggling with this question even for ministry purposes in order to be able to spread the gospel. First of all, I do want to make clear that at the time of this writing, this is not the mark of the beast yet; through my personal Bible study, I do see it leading to the "Mark" and contributing to the infrastructure of the antichrist and his eventual "Mark." Every Christian is going to have to make their own personal decision. The personal and social pressure that is attached to this decision for many has become divisive.

I do see even this contemplation as a parallel to the future "Mark." What I mean is, in the near future, there will be those that are going to come under tremendous pressure from every direction and even rationalize taking the actual "Mark." Compromise with evil for the "greater good" is never blessed by God in any decision. This vaccine parallel's the "Mark" in many ways, even the pressure and coercion to take it. I find this element, as well as other factors, very evil.

What I really want to convey here is; whether you have taken this shot or not, we as Christians need to wake up and recognize what satan is trying to do. Though I, myself, am not vaccinated, nor ever will be vaccinated. I don't want to alienate my family and friends who are Christians that have taken this particular shot. We all still have a purpose in fighting the evil in these last days. It's not too late for any of us to stand in solidarity together in order to fight this physical and now spiritual battle against the evil of our day that's in high gear in developing the antichrist system. It's on the fast track.

It's our obligation as Christians to fight evil when we see it. We as Christians should not be silent or capitulate in ways that give power to what satan is trying to accomplish. If you're a vaccinated Christian who now realizes the lies and where they are heading. You can still fight the ongoing antichrist system and protect yourself by making wiser decisions going forward in reference to boosters and other shots that they will be pushing on you. Though you may qualify for a vaccine passport on your cell phone in order to enjoy some luxuries; you don't have to get one; in doing so, you are giving power to the eventual development of the Mark of the Beast and the antichrist system, not to mention you will have to continue to get future booster shots to keep your vaccine passport active. This is the hook; to reward you with freedoms that they took away that were already yours, to begin with. You will also be added to another tracking database that will be used to monitor you. Next, they will want you to have a passport on your right hand or forehead. I hope you can see how they are stair-stepping mankind at a fast pace into this demonic direction globally; that after relinquishing all your individual liberties, you will be forced into an economic religious system that will require you to be "marked" like a slave and forever changed and condemned. We are living through the development of the lie now being perpetrated on humanity through a series of lies that will end at the ultimate lie, the "mark."

Two things I know for sure about this current pandemic. (1. The Corona Virus is real, and (2. Their solutions are a complete lie, and they don't appear interested in real solutions that would save lives; as a matter of fact, real solutions are censored or canceled. It would be nice if you could go to your local doctor at the onset of corona to get medications to treat you. This one simple, practical solution could cause those to avoid urgent care hospital visits. Most hospitals aren't following the best protocols presently to save lives, and these protocols need to be changed as well. There are several medications available now, but our government will not allow your local doctors to prescribe. Why not? These are the same people that do not value life. This is an evil mess we are in right now. This is all leading towards global governance, total control, and the mark of the beast.

Let me make it clear; no one has taken the Mark of the Beast yet, and I pray that none of my family and friends will in the future. We all need to continue to educate ourselves, especially spiritually. Once we are able to look past the tree in front of us, we will be able to see the entire forest. Pride and fear need to be put aside, and the spiritual armor put on. The Bible says, *"for the lack of knowledge my people perish"* Hosea 4:6.

"No weapon formed against you shall prosper, And every tongue which rises against you in judgment You shall condemn. This is the heritage of the servants of the Lord, And their righteousness is from Me," Says the Lord." Isaiah 54:17 NKJV

This verse is telling us that we are to fight and push back against every evil regardless of any backlash. It's our right, and God commands us to do so!

As the church here in America, I firmly believe we need to wake up, stand together in solidarity, forget about the 501c3 status being lost and start pushing back against this particular lie fiercely here in the United States while we still have some freedoms to do so. Pastors preach about revival and pray that revival will come to our land. These past couple of years have revealed who the cold, hot, and lukewarm churches are. Unfortunately for the hot churches in which are few, they don't have the solidarity and support of most churches right now. The cold churches are entirely sold out to the government and their edicts. While It seems there are many lukewarm churches in our day straddling the line between pretending to be bold while appeasing the government simultaneously. Most evangelical churches fall into this category today. As large as we are in this country, if we were hot, we wouldn't have the problems we are having right now.

Along with every Christian magazine sent out to pastors, many high profile Christians have pushed and convinced churches to play along with a government that has oppressed and created mandates that directly oppose God's will for the church as well as attack and separate the families. For example, the obedient church would not allow their doors to be closed, Revelation 3:8, Hebrews 10:25.

I know we thought at first we were doing the right thing, but it has become clear that this response is all deception, every bit of it, but their boards are pressuring churches to continue to play along. This will not end until we start pushing back, especially with the evil running rampant in our country today.

"And Elijah came to all the people, and said, "How long will you falter between two opinions? If the LORD is God, follow Him; but if Baal, follow him." But the people answered him not a word."
I Kings 18:21 NKJV

I believe this passage describes the state of the Church perfectly right now. We are at a spiritual crossroads. We are ripe for a revival to break out across this country and the world right now. Who will the Church follow? Are we seeing through the circumstances today the beginning of the great apostasy?

Pastors and churches need to be an opposition voice. It will start a huge revival here for the rest of the world to marvel at if we would. God has handed it to us on a silver platter for the taking! We need to step out on faith and trust God. We and our country will be better for it. Christians in our historical past have always led our nation through and out of difficult times. But it's like we are waiting on the most vital circumstances before we act. Unfortunately, that's what appears the Bible indicates as well.

We as Christians shouldn't give up our rights for the "greater good" to be a neighbor. This is another false doctrine of demons intended to keep the Church stagnant, separated, and ineffective for the kingdom, allowing evil to prevail with little to no resistance. Fear brings about manipulation. These rights that Christians were told to give up in our recent past are God-given rights that are also proceeded by our U.S. Constitution. Lost people are seeking answers, and they recognize that something isn't right. The Church needs to be bold proclaimers of truth, not advocates of deception! We need to stand up for righteousness as the apostles of Christ did! We cannot allow what happened before to happen again. It's time to get out of our comfort zones.

*"**not forsaking the assembling of ourselves together**, as is the manner of some, but exhorting one another, and **so much the more as you see the Day approaching.**" Hebrews 10:25 NKJV*

This is a commandment to the Church, especially the Endtime Church. We need to assemble and encourage one another in the face of deception, hardship, persecution, and darkness as we stand up for what is right during these last days. The Bible says so! This is the kind of faith that attracts people to the Truth. Be Bold and Love your neighbor! Wake up, Church of Laodicea, wake up!

The Good news is that this all means Jesus is coming back soon! Within the coming years, we may very well be in the midst of the final seven-year period, with all of this coming to a victorious conclusion shortly. Until then, Christians of the United States, let us be the beacon of hope for all of the world to see.

The Bible says to abide until his arrival. God birth this country on this planet as the greatest Christian nation to ever exist. It's our responsibility to care for what He has given to us. Have we been doing a good job? Our country has been on a dark path for a while now. There is still hope, and we must take seriously the times in which we are presently living. It's time to wake up! We need to be praying while at the same time taking action. Let us and the United States of America be mighty adversaries of the evil of our day and what it's trying to accomplish. I know most of you have been taught that the United States doesn't exist in Endtime Bible prophecy. I'm here to tell you that couldn't be further from the truth. We will be adversaries of the antichrist and his global government, but it needs to start right now!

The second question asked in my introduction was, "Where is all of this leading?" The answer is that it's leading to Jesus Christ's return for his Church! The rapture!

Ephesians 5:11

Days of Noah and The Rapture

*"37**But as the days of Noah were, so also will the coming of the Son of Man be**. 38For as in the days before the flood, they were eating and drinking, marrying and giving in marriage, until the day that Noah entered the ark, 39and did not know until the flood came and took them all away, so also will the coming of the Son of Man be." Matthew 24:37-39*

As I have shown you in the previous chapter, without a doubt, we are living in the days of Noah, and it's leading to the Rapture and Jesus' 2nd coming. The reflection moment made in Revelation 18:23 couldn't be a clearer depiction of what we are going through worldwide right now; we are living in that moment. This is a massive indicator of how close we are. It's incredible to see Bible prophecy being fulfilled right before our eyes in real-time! It really should build your faith in the scriptures and the reality that it will not be long before our Lord Jesus comes to receive us unto Himself in the clouds!

So in this chapter, we will be discussing the rapture as it relates to the Days of Noah. We will also be bringing in other passages from the Bible to qualify and connect a few dots to the days leading right up to the day of the flood. Jesus tells us plainly that his coming would be like the Days of Noah. We have already discussed the evil of the day and how satan used his angels to bring about a race of evil demonic beings that influenced mankind's heart to ponder on evil continuously that caused God to bring about the flood. Some believe that this is all there is to glean from Noah's days in relation to the environment of the time of the rapture. Again I will be sharing with you some things you probably haven't heard or been taught before. There is much more to glean from the Days of Noah as it relates directly to the rapture itself that most either ignore because it doesn't fit their traditional teaching or they just have overlooked it without a proper understanding of what they were reading. So let's begin.

*1Then the Lord said to Noah, "***Come into the ark***, you and all your household, because I have seen that* ***you are righteous before Me in this generation.*** *2You shall take with you seven each of every clean animal, a male and his female; two each of animals that are unclean, a male and his female; 3also seven each of birds of the air, male and female, to keep the species alive on the face of all the earth. 4***For after seven more days** *I will cause it to rain on the earth forty days and forty nights, and I will destroy from the face of the earth all living things that I have made." 5And Noah did according to all that the Lord* **commanded** *him. 6Noah was* **six hundred years old** *when the floodwaters were on the earth.*
Genesis 7:1-6 NKJV

So there is quite a bit to unpack from this passage of scripture. As a backdrop, Noah had been building the Ark for approximately 120 years. We got this information from Genesis 6:3 when God stated that his Spirit wouldn't strive with man forever and at that time gave Noah detailed instructions to start building the Ark. Here in this passage, Noah is finished building the Ark, however, is given some final instructions right before the flood.

First, Noah is instructed to
"Come into the Ark." The Ark represents safety and security; in essence, the Ark represents Salvation for Noah and his family. God tells Noah that the reason he can come into the Ark is that *"you are righteous before Me in this generation."* For Noah, he was living during the end of time during an evil generation. Much like we are today. So by comparison, the parallel that can be made to our present generation from these first two highlights are that Jesus is the "Ark of Salvation," and those that have a relationship with Jesus are considered the righteous ones before him worthy to be saved from God's final wrath on the planet.

The second point to be made I find fascinating and the most overlooked. Noah is given a task to make sure that the animals are correctly gathered into the Ark. Noah is also given a final timeline in which this is needed to be done before God's wrath would come by the floodwaters *"for after seven more days."* Noah was told by God ahead of time the very day of his departure and when the wrath of God would begin. This is amazing! I want to remind you once again what Jesus stated in Matthew.

*"37**But as the days of Noah were, so also will the coming of the Son of Man be**. Matthew 24:37 NKJV*

Ok, so you are probably asking yourself right now, are you insinuating that we will know the Day of the rapture? The simple answer would be, Noah knew. The endtime generation has already been given the same kind of timeline that Noah was given. Once this timeline commences, we will know how much longer we will have left here, just like Noah knew. When will this happen? The seven-day timeline that we, as the endtime Church, have been given is mentioned in the book of Daniel. This is also how we will know when it starts.

*27Then **he shall confirm a covenant with many for one week**; But in the middle of the week He shall bring an end to sacrifice and offering. And on the wing of abominations shall be one who makes desolate, Even until the consummation, which is determined, Is poured out on the desolate." Daniel 9:27 NKJV*

"He shall confirm a covenant with many for one week" The "he" here is the antichrist. The antichrist will be confirming a covenant between Israel and many other nations, including the Palestinian people. The length of this covenant will last "one symbolic week," this is a week of years, not days, with each day representing a year. Our departure will be on the same day as Noah's departure. The seventh day (or 7th year in our case). One may ask, how do you know this covenant is actually

seven years and not seven days? Let's take a look at the rest of this verse and connect some dots with other passages of scripture to get this answer. It states in Daniel that the antichrist in the middle of the week will bring an end to the sacrifice and offerings, and in turn, will commit the abominations who makes desolate. So, as a result of this covenant, we know that a 3rd Jewish temple will have to be built; otherwise, the antichrist wouldn't be able to stop offerings and sacrifices or commit the abominations of desolation in it (proclaim himself as god). The last time the Jews had a temple on the temple mount was 2,000 years ago. Jesus in Matthew chapter 24 refers to Daniel 9:27 as an indication as to when the Great Tribulation will start.

15"Therefore when you see the ***'abomination of desolation,' spoken of by Daniel the prophet****, standing in the holy place" (whoever reads, let him understand)…….21****For then there will be great tribulation****, such as has not been since the beginning of the world until this time, no, nor ever shall be. Matthew 24:15, 21 NKJV*

When did Jesus say the Great Tribulation will start? Answer: when we see the abomination of desolation spoken of by Daniel. When did Daniel say this event was going to happen? Answer: in the middle of the week (3 1/2 days). How long will the Great Tribulation last?
3 1/2 days (3 1/2 years). We know that the Great Tribulation is 3 1/2 years because there are several places in the Bible that state that the antichrist is only granted authority for
3 1/2 years, for example:

5And he was given a mouth speaking great things and blasphemies, and he was given authority to continue for ***forty-two months****. Revelation 13:5 NKJV*

Forty-two months is the same as 3 1/2 years, the length of the Great Tribulation. So, in conclusion, from this, we know that the entire week of Daniel 9:27 is actually seven years.

I want to pause in order to highlight something. The first 3 1/2 years is not the Great Tribulation; it doesn't start until the mid-point. Some call the entire seven-year period the "the 7-year tribulation" The correct name for the seven-year time frame should be called "Daniel's 70th week" (Daniel 9:24-27). Some also call the entire seven-year period "Jacob's time of trouble," however, in Jeremiah 30:7, he refers to the Great Tribulation in the same way Jesus did in Matthew 24:21 when Jesus referred to Daniel as the time when the Great Tribulation will begin. "Jacob's Time of Trouble" starts at the midpoint of the final seven-year time frame, not at the beginning. We have the connections between Jeremiah, Daniel, and Jesus all saying the same thing; the Great Tribulation will begin at the mid-point of Daniel's 70th week (final seven year period). The only places the word "tribulation" is spoken of in the new testament as a reference to the endtime is when Jesus speaks of tribulation and "Great Tribulation," which occurs during the 2nd half of the final seven years. Those that believe in the popular pre-tribulation rapture view adhere to the terminology of a seven-year tribulation because they have to for it to fit their traditional flawed idea of the timing of the rapture; otherwise, they would be putting themselves being raptured approximately 3 1/2 years into the final seven-year period when the Great Tribulation actually begins. This is just one of many flaws with the pre-tribulation rapture view.

The third point: God's wrath during the Days of Noah didn't occur until the 7th day. God's wrath during the final seven years will not happen until the 7th year. Traditional teaching is that the entire final seven-year period is God's wrath being poured out on humanity, and because Christians are not appointed unto God's wrath, we will be raptured before it begins. Though we as Christians aren't appointed unto God's wrath, the mistake made by scholars and pastors are in the details and understanding of God's word concerning this topic matter. Some coin the phrase, why would God beat his bride before the wedding? God will not beat his bride but instead will be receiving a spiritually beautiful bride that will endure till the end like Noah. The absolute truth here is that the "Great Tribulation" is not God's wrath; it's Satan's wrath. There are several passages to show this; here is an example of one.

25He shall speak pompous words against the Most High, Shall persecute the saints of the Most High,
And shall intend to change times and law.
Then the saints shall be given into his hand
For a time and times and half a time
(3 1/2 years)*.... Daniel 7:25 NKJV*

Let me be abundantly clear the
"Great Tribulation" is not the wrath of God; it's the wrath of satan. God's wrath does not begin until the very end of the seven-year period. The seven bowls are filled up with the
"wrath of God." Most of the wrath of God is poured out at the "Battle of Armageddon."

*1Then I heard a loud voice from the temple saying to the seven angels, "Go and pour out the **bowls of the wrath of God** on the earth." 2So the **first went and poured out his bowl** upon the earth, and a foul and loathsome sore came upon the men who had the **mark of the beast** and those who **worshiped his image.** Revelation 16:1-2 NKJV*

The first bowl will not be poured out until the mark of the beast is administered. This gives us a timeline of when these Bowls start. We know that the antichrist is revealed globally at the Abomination of Desolation, which is at the 3 1/2 year point (midpoint) of the final seven-year period. It's likely that the mark of the beast will not be implemented until sometime during the final 7th year towards the end of the antichrist 42 months or 3 1/2 reign. This also coincides with the Days of Noah and the timing of God's wrath by flood, which began on the 7th day. We as Christians will not suffer from God's wrath due to these Bowls. We now, as Christians, are sealed by God for protection. Revelation says that the 144,000 will be sealed for protection. God seals anyone up until that point who has given their life to Christ for his protection until the one and only day of redemption, the rapture!

13In Him you also trusted, after you heard the word of truth, the gospel of your salvation; in whom also, having believed, ***you were sealed with the Holy Spirit*** *of promise, 14who is the guarantee of our inheritance* ***until the redemption of the purchased possession,*** *to the praise of His glory. Ephesians 1:13-14 NKJV*

Now that we have established that we will have the same parallel timeline as Noah had during the last days of his generation. We also know that Noah was given notice ahead of time of the day of his departure. We, too, like Noah, will be departing or raptured on the same day (7th day or year). As we continue to look at Genesis 7:1-6, we find that Noah did what the Lord had "commanded" him to do during his final seven days. We, too, will have a purpose during the final seven years. Our purpose and mission will be much the same as it has always been, however with much more urgency because we will know our time is short. Our "command" will be to continue the "Great Commission" during the "Great Tribulation" and guide people into the Ark of salvation who is Jesus Christ. This will be a time of the Greatest Revival this world has ever seen! It will be the best of times and worst of times all at the same time.

18And Jesus came and spoke to them, saying, "All authority has been given to Me in heaven and on earth. 19Go therefore and make disciples of all the nations, baptizing them in the name of the Father and of the Son and of the Holy Spirit, 20teaching them to observe all things that I have commanded you; and lo, I am with you always, ***even to the end of the age.****" Amen. Matthew 28:18-20 NKJV*

The 4th and final point from this passage in Genesis people overlook or don't give much thought to is amazing as well. It states that Noah was 600 years old when the floodwaters came upon the earth.

6Noah was ***six hundred years old*** *when the floodwaters were on the earth. Genesis 7:6 NKJV*

You may be asking what is so significant about this? It's another parallel to the times in which we are living now. You see, according to the Bible genealogy, the earth is approaching 6,000 years old right now. How do we arrive at this Biblical date? The genealogies of Genesis 5 and 11 make it clear that Abraham lived about 2,000 years after the creation. And we know from chronologies found elsewhere in the Bible that Abraham lived about 2,000 years before the birth of Jesus Christ. Furthermore, we know that Jesus' ministry was about 2,000 years ago. Summing these lengths of time, we get about 6,000 years. I gathered this information directly from *answersingenesis.org*.

God carefully coordinated the age of Noah at 600 of his departure during the flood with earth's age at the time of the Rapture at earth's 6,000th year! This is unbelievable, people! It gets even more amazing. Let's look at 2Peter 3:8-9

8But, beloved, do not forget this one thing, ***that with the Lord one day is as a thousand years, and a thousand years as one day.*** *9The Lord is not slack concerning His promise, as some count slackness, but is longsuffering toward us, not willing that any should perish but that all should come to repentance.*
2Peter 3:8-9 NKJV

The backdrop of this passage here in 2nd Peter references the "Day of the Lord," end of times. Not only does God parallel the Days of Noah with the timing of the rapture of the Church, however, the days of creation themselves, with each day representing a thousand years. God rested on the 7th day of creation. We are quickly approaching earth's 6,000th year that will be preceded by Daniel's 70th week or the final seven years. The following one thousand years will be Jesus Christ Millennium reign on earth. During the 1,000-year millennium, Jesus will have created a new refurbished heaven and earth for his followers to enjoy with complete peace without the presence of sin. This will happen during earth's 7,000th year, coinciding with the 7th day of creation, the day that God took rest. In reading through the Bible, God is very calculating in the things he does and the timing in which he does them. This is so amazing! The Bible is so Real, Living, and Breathing! We are the generation He chose to live through this time. Jesus is coming back soon! Though we are coming to the end of this age, don't rest just yet, we still have work to do!

Here in Genesis, it shows us a picture of the rapture during the time of Noah and his household.

17Now the flood was on the earth forty days. The waters increased and ***lifted up the ark****, and it* ***rose high above the earth****. Genesis 7:17 NKJV*

As Noah and his family are being rescued and rising into the heavens while in the Ark, at the same time, all the wicked people are being destroyed on earth.

Here is Jesus speaking about the time of the end using the account of Lot and his household.

*29but the **same day** that Lot went out of Sodom it rained fire and brimstone from heaven and destroyed them all. 30**Even so will it be** in the day when the Son of Man is revealed. Luke 17:29-30 KJV*

The correlation between Noah and Lot is that there are absolutely no second chances for anyone left behind. Furthermore, Noah was given a final seven days to get all the animals into the Ark before the flood destroyed everything. When the Daniel 9:27 covenant is confirmed, this will commence the household of Christ (Christians) a final seven days (years) to fulfill the commandment of the Great Commission set by Jesus found in
Matthew 28:18-20, afterward, we are raptured.

Now let me finally address the **elephant** in the room :) You have probably been asking yourself, doesn't the Bible say no one will know the day or hour of Jesus' return? The scripture most often referred to when asking this question is found in Matthew 24:36.

36"But of that day and hour no one knows, not even the angels of heaven, but My Father only.
Matthew 24:36 NKJV

Some argue that Jesus was only speaking to those in the first century and not people presently. Also, some would say that Jesus being God is all-knowing and would have had to know himself when answering this question, but instead, he stated only the Father. Jesus, while on earth, did humble himself as a man while also being God. Now, he is sitting at the right hand of the Father in his full glory, so I'm pretty sure Jesus knows now when he is returning. For example, when Jesus was in heaven speaking with John, I find it very interesting the words Jesus chose to use in Revelation 3:3.

Remember therefore how you have received and heard; hold fast and repent. Therefore ***if you will not watch****, I will come upon you as a thief, and you will not know what hour I will come upon you. Revelation 3:3 NKJV*

Did you catch this? Jesus is clearly telling us to be watchful; in doing so, the assertion is made that we could even know the hour of his return! So what do we do with this? Let's continue to search the scriptures.

34Assuredly, I say to you, this generation will by no means pass away till all these things take place. Matthew 24:34 NKJV

The generation being referred to here is the endtime generation. We are the generation that was given all the signs and warnings to watch for, for example, wars, rumors of wars, famines, pestilences, and even the antichrist's rise to power. In *(1 Thessalonians 5:1-5)*, Paul clearly tells us we will have an advantage on timelines as time draws nearer.

1But concerning the times and the seasons, brethren, you have no need that I should write to you. 2For you yourselves know perfectly that the day of the Lord so comes as a thief in the night. 3For when they say, "Peace and safety!" then sudden destruction comes upon them, as labor pains upon a pregnant woman. And they shall not escape. ***4But you, brethren, are not in darkness, so that this Day should overtake you as a thief. 5You are all sons of light and sons of the day.*** *We are not of the night nor of darkness.*
1 Thessalonians 5:1-5 NKJV

Again we see the same terminology of Revelation 3:3. Once again, we are told that we will have an advantage over the lost people (in darkness). The "Day of the Lord" would not overtake us like a thief because we are children of light and sons of the day. The "Day of the Lord" is the rapture. Let's continue.

*42**Watch** therefore, for you do not know what hour your Lord is coming. 43But know this, that if the master of the house had known what hour the thief would come, he would have **watched** and not allowed his house to be broken into. 44Therefore you also **be ready**, for the Son of Man is coming at an hour you do not expect. Matthew 24:42-44 NKJV*

The "thief" represents the lord here, and the "master" represents unbelievers. The master lives in darkness and is not ready for the coming of the lord. The Church is told here more than once to be watching. Furthermore, Paul clarifies in *(1 Thessalonians 5:4-5)* that we are children of light, and the darkness wouldn't overtake us like the thief. If we stay in our Bibles and follow current events, we will know that the time is drawing nearer, even at the doorstep. Paul also explains Jesus 2nd coming like birth pangs in *(1 Thessalonians 5:3)*. When contractions are minutes apart, you're not nine months out anymore; you're in the delivery room. I don't claim to know the day or the hour, but I know we will soon know the DAY. The Bible has always been our navigational tool for life, and it will continue to be so during these last days. This is why we have the prophetic scriptures that consist of almost one-third of the Bible. God could have ended the Bible any way he wanted; however, he chose to end it with a book dedicated to end time Bible prophecy, the book of Revelation. It states at the beginning of Revelation that anyone who reads and understands would be blessed. We are told to be watchers; keep watching!

I want to end our study back at the "Days of Noah" with the passage we first began our study with.

*"37But as the days of Noah were, so also will the coming of the Son of Man be. 38**For as in the days before the flood, they were eating and drinking, marrying and giving in marriage, until the day that Noah entered the ark**, 39and did not know until the flood came and took them all away, **so also will the coming of the Son of Man be.**" Matthew 24:37-39*

After everything we have discussed and discovered in the Bible, one may still ask, I thought the rapture would come like in the Days of Noah? Everyone eating, drinking and having a good time, etc... How could this environment be happening at the end of the tribulation period with all the chaos and destruction on the earth during that time? Wouldn't this type of environment only exist before the final seven years start? These are all great questions. Yes, this type of environment would certainly exist prior to the final seven years beginning. This type of environment existed before Noah's final seven-day instructions prior to the flood, yet Noah's departure and the flood didn't occur until the 7th day. One amazing thing I've discovered is, Bible prophecy answers Bible prophecy. To better answer these questions, let's go to the scriptures and see what is happening at the end of the tribulation period.

"When they finish their testimony, the beast that ascends out of the bottomless pit will make war against them, overcome them, and kill them............Then those from the peoples, tribes, tongues, and nations will see their dead bodies three-and-a- half days, and not allow their dead bodies to be put into graves. ***And those who dwell on the earth will rejoice over them, make merry, and send gifts to one another****, because these two prophets tormented those who dwell on the earth." Revelation 11:7, 9-10 NKJV*

Here in Revelation 11 are exactly what Jesus describes from Matthew found happening after the two witnesses (**prophets**) are killed. Are the dots starting to connect? Watch what happens next.

11And after three days and an half the Spirit of life from God entered into them, and they stood upon their feet; and great fear fell upon them which saw them. 12And they heard a great voice from heaven saying unto them, ***Come up hither****. And they* ***ascended up to heaven in a cloud****; and their enemies beheld them. Revelation 11:11-12 KJV*

These two witnesses ascend to heaven from the earth in a cloud, and their enemies beheld them. Remember, the Bible says the dead in Christ will rise first.

.....And the dead in Christ will rise first. 17Then we which are alive and remain shall be ***caught up together with them in the clouds****, to meet the Lord in the air: and so shall we ever be with the Lord. 1Thessalonians 4:16-17 KJV*

*7****Behold, he cometh with clouds; and every eye shall see him****, and they also which pierced him: and all kindreds of the earth shall wail because of him. Even so, Amen. Revelation 1:7 KJV*

Both of these passages state we will meet Jesus in the clouds among witnesses. These two witnesses ascended to heaven, just like Jesus did. This is the time of the rapture. Also, If you look further down in chapter 11 of Revelation, it states that in that **same hour** is when the final 7th Trumpet sounds. The last Trumpet!

51Behold, I tell you a mystery: We shall not all sleep, but we shall all be changed— 52in a moment, in the twinkling of an eye, ***at the last trumpet****. For the trumpet will sound, and the dead will be raised incorruptible, and we shall be changed.*
1st Corinthians 15:51-52 NKJV

There is one last point I would like to make, remember earlier when we discussed the correct terminology for the final seven-year period? "Jacob's Time of Trouble" is one of the proper titles for the "Great Tribulation" which occurs at the mid-point of the final seven-year period. Let's look at the passage that corroborates this.

7Alas! For that day is great, So that none is like it; And it is the ***time of Jacob's trouble****, But* ***he shall be saved out of it.*** *Jeremiah 30:7 NKJV*

This scripture parallels Matthew 24:21, a passage we referenced earlier when Jesus was speaking. Do you see what I see? It plainly states, *"he shall be saved out of it"* (A picture of the Rapture). The simple point here is that you can't be saved out of something that you're not already in. Jacob's time of trouble (Great Tribulation), and we are saved out of it (Raptured). It's plainly spoken. By the way for those that say that Jeremiah is only referencing the Jews; there is only one rapture not many, and when Jesus returns he will be coming back for a Jewish/Gentile church mix just like it was in the early church.

Be Ready! Be Bold! Be Brave! Without Fear!

The "Days of Noah," what did Jesus say again?

*37****But as the days of Noah were, so also will the coming of the Son of Man be****. Matthew 24:37 NKJV*

Enter the Ark

Someone reading this book may be wondering how can I make sure that I'm saved from the wrath that is to come? Let me be the one to tell you that Jesus is the Ark of Salvation, and he is the lover of your soul; he alone is the only one that can save you if you are willing to accept his invitation.

Jesus says: *"I am the Truth the Way and the Life" John 14:*6

To really appreciate the good news of the gospel, we have to first be willing to face the reality of the bad news of what Jesus is saving us from.

The bad news is that humanity is infected with something much worse than corona; it's called sin. Sin is what separates us from God and the relationship he desires to have with us through his son Jesus Christ. Without this relationship, we are already condemned to a place of torment that was never created for humankind but was designed for satan and all of his fallen angels. So what must we do? A person must first acknowledge that they have sinned; you must realize you are a sinner who needs a savior. You must **acknowledge** your sinful condition and understand that Jesus alone is your only solution.

"For all have sinned and come short of the glory of God" Romans 3:23 NKJV

"There is none righteous, no, not one"
Romans 3:10 NKJV

You cannot save yourself.

For by grace you have been saved through faith, ***and that not of yourselves; it is the gift of God,*** *9not of works, lest anyone should boast.*
Ephesians 2:8-9 NKJV

You must **believe** that Jesus died on the cross for your sins and rose the 3rd day from the dead as the victory over your sin.

16For God so loved the world that He gave His only begotten Son, that whoever ***believes in Him*** *should not perish but have everlasting life. 17For God did not send His Son into the world to condemn the world, but that the world through Him might be saved.*
John 3:16-17 NKJV

Next, you need to **confess** that you're a sinner to Jesus himself and ask him to come into your life to be Lord, Savior, and Ruler.

9that if you ***confess*** *with your mouth the Lord Jesus and* ***believe*** *in your heart that God has raised Him from the dead, you will be saved. 10For with the heart one* ***believes*** *unto righteousness, and with the mouth* ***confession*** *is made unto salvation.*
Romans 10:9-10 NKJV

You could pray something like this in your own words straight from your heart.

Lord Jesus I know that I'm a sinner and I ask forgiveness of my sins. I believe you died on the cross and rose the third day so I could receive your forgiveness and eternal life. I ask that you come into my life and be my Lord and Savior. I give you control over my life and ask that you help me to live for you from this day forward. Amen.

If you have just given your life to Jesus Christ, your name is written in the Lambs Book of Life, and his Holy Spirit has Sealed you for eternity, and the angels in heaven are rejoicing now over your decision. You have just entered into the Ark of Jesus and the Salvation that he has promised!

10Likewise, I say to you, there is joy in the presence of the angels of God over one sinner who repents."
Luke 15:10 NKJV

Your Purpose in life is simple; don't live by fear, instead go out as the victorious Christian you are and be the light of Christ in this dark world for everyone around you to see, for Jesus Is coming soon!

14"You are the light of the world. A city that is set on a hill cannot be hidden. 15Nor do they light a lamp and put it under a basket, but on a lampstand, and it gives light to all who are in the house. 16Let your light so shine before men, that they may see your good works and glorify your Father in heaven.
Matthew 5:14-16 NKJV

Find yourself a Bible-believing church for community. Though baptism is not a requirement for salvation; it symbolizes outwardly much like a wedding band does that you now have a relationship with Jesus; your baptism is a great witness for those lost.

God chose you to live through this Biblically prophetic time in history for his glory! He wouldn't have allowed you to be born during these times that will soon lead to his return if he didn't think you were capable of shining for him. He sees greatness in you! He sees greatness in the remnant of his Church!

C. S. DeCaro

If you haven't already, I encourage you to read my book ***"The Endtime is Now: According to the Bible, Be Ready!"***. This book provides a more in-depth look into the times in which we are living. As events continue to unfold, the understanding of Bible prophecy is becoming more clear and easier to understand by the day. All the dots are connecting presently. God told Daniel that it would be like this during the time of the end.

8Although I heard, I did not understand. Then I said, "My lord, what shall be the end of these things?" 9And he said, "Go your way, Daniel, for the words are closed up and sealed ***till the time of the end.*** *10Many shall be purified, made white, and refined, but the wicked shall do wickedly; and none of the wicked shall understand,* ***but the wise shall understand****.*
Daniel 12:8-10 NKJV

That Time is Now. Be Ready!

Available: Paperback & E-book

Resources

New King James Version Bible, NKJV

New American Standard Bible, NASB

https://www.bible.com Bible App (It's Free!)

Blue Letter Bible
https://www.blueletterbible.org (Used for original Greek Strong's concordance) (It's Free!)

Answers In Genesis
https://answersingenesis.org/age-of-the-earth/how-old-earth/

Modified cover image
Image by Hany Alashkar from Pixabay

The Endtime is Now: According to the Bible, Be Ready!

Facts are true whether one wants to believe them or not. I'm going to share with you some hard truth so that you may know that you have been lied to. I hope this hard but factual truth will embolden you to take a stand against the deception and evil of our day. Though I could show you countless documentation, I'm only going to share with you one that comes from a FDA/CDC co-managed website. This database was established in 1990 and is updated every Friday with a two-week lag. It's called OpenVaers; it's a **V**accine **A**dverse **E**ffect **R**eporting **S**ystem. The reports received are from medical providers of patients that have had adverse effects directly from a vaccine here in the United States. The numbers you will see are only a fraction of all events because not all medical providers take the time to submit such detailed reports; however, these numbers alone are enough that this covid19 vaccine should be pulled off the market ASAP, much less mandated. I encourage you to navigate this site, also know that each statistic is clickable for a further breakdown of details for a particular number. You do not hear this from the media or most of your elected officials though the data is easily accessible for anyone to see. You will be shocked!

https://openvaers.com/covid-data

Printed in Great Britain
by Amazon

79410026R00037